I Am
Kamala Harris

Maryann Cusimano Love and Maria Love

GLOBAL
COLLECTIVE
PUBLISHERS

As soon as I could stand, I began standing up for justice. When I was a toddler my parents took me to Civil Rights marches, in California, where I was born. People sang joyful songs of freedom. They painted signs saying "Love your Neighbor," "Freedom," and "Equal Justice Under the Law." People of every color and background were kind to each other, working together to make the American Dream come true for everybody. It was like a rainbow parade for fairness. I loved it.

Once, I slipped out of my stroller at a march. My mother hugged me to comfort my fussing.

"What do you want, baby?" she asked.

"Fweedom!" I answered, just like the other civil rights marchers.

The family laughed. But I meant it.

My favorite book was "The Lion, the Witch and the Wardrobe." In the story, children suffer from war, and there's a long spell of darkness over the land. The leader, the evil white witch, doesn't help people, and fights against what's right.

A young girl leads the children to defeat the evil. They are brave, work together, have faith, and make a better world.

I wanted to be like those children.

All shall be done, but it may be harder than you think.

Are you brave again?

In our adversity, God shouts to us.

May your wisdom grace us until the stars rain down from the heavens.

I have come home at last! This is my country! I belong here...
Come further up, come further in!

Courage, dear heart, Dearest daughter

They Open A Door And Enter A World.

The Lion, the Witch and the Wardrobe
C. S. LEWIS

My parents worked hard to make a better world.

My mother, Shyamala Gopalan, came from India to study in America, at a time when it was hard for girls to go to University.

My mother became a scientist who worked to find a cure for breast cancer. We always called her Mommy. Sometimes she let my sister Maya and I help her in the lab.

My father, Donald Harris, came from Jamaica to study in California. He became a University professor, who taught about fighting poverty.

Some people treated my parents badly, because they had dark skin, because they spoke with accents, because they were immigrants. But my parents worked hard.

Mommy always said, "Whatever you learn, use it to help others."

My babysitter, Mrs. Shelton, had a picture in her home of a lawyer named Thurgood Marshall, who fought so that all children would have the chance to learn. I wanted to be a lawyer like Thurgood Marshall, who helped people.

In first grade I rode the Red Rooster school bus. It was a special bus. It took people like me with dark skin, to go to school together with kids who had light skin.

Some did not welcome us.
Some white parents would not let their kids play with us.

I like learning.
On the Red Rooster, I learned
that the best thing to do with an enemy is to
turn them into a friend. We played Cats Cradle,
Miss Mary Mack, and sang Michael Jackson songs.

I drew Indian henna patterns on my new friends' hands.

I learned I could make friends with people who did not look like me.

When I learned to write, the first thing I did was write a letter to the President. I asked him to stop the war in Vietnam because it was hurting people.

In third grade my parents divorced. This made me sad. So I learned to cheer myself up. Mommy taught me how to crochet and how to cook.

Some of my favorites are Idli, Sambar, and Tikka. But my specialty is scrambled eggs topped with cheese smiley faces. I like cooking; it's a gift you can give people.

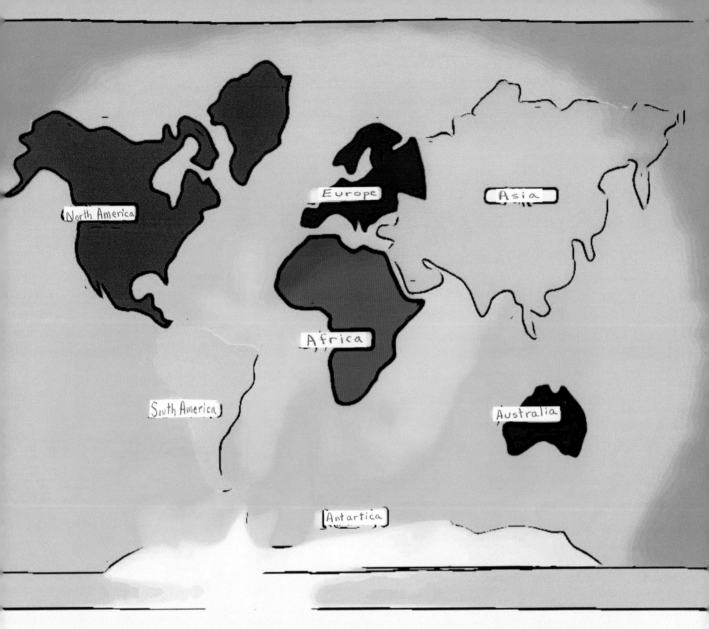

In geography class, I showed the teacher places I had been. My teacher did not believe me; she told my mother I was making up stories. Mommy explained to the teacher that we had traveled to India, Jamaica, and Zambia, and to my mother's international work meetings. I learned that good people all over the world are standing up to make a better future.

I also learned that kids need adults who listen and believe in them.

At school, a boy was bullying a girl. Whenever I complained to Mommy about something that wasn't right, she always said, "Well, what are you going to do about it?"

I thought about that. When the bully threw my friend's craft project on the ground, I told him to stop. He hit me. I was bleeding so much I had to go to the hospital. And I learned that fighting was not the answer.

When I was twelve, we moved to Canada, so my mother could keep working to try to cure cancer. I missed sunny California. And the owner of our apartment building would not let children play on the lawn. That wasn't fair. Kids have rights too! All people need to go outside and exercise. I organized the kids, just like my parents' civil rights marches.

Because we stood up, the owner changed the rule, and we played soccer on the lawn.

I went to high school, where I learned French, played violin, French horn, kettle drum, and danced. The musician, Leonard Cohen, who wrote a famous song, "Hallelujah," also went to the same school, years before me.

I missed my elder neighbors back home in the U.S., so I started a dance
group called "Midnight Madness." We played at Senior Centers, and brought
a lot of smiles. One of my friends in the group was being hurt by her
stepfather, so I stood up for her. She came and lived with my family.

I went to the college that my hero Thurgood Marshall graduated from.

I stood up for other students in need, and started a mentoring program.

I became a lawyer, and headed the Children's and Family Services Department. Other lawyers looked down on this work; they called it "kiddie law." But children need adults who will stand up for them. My first day on the job I arrived with my arms full of teddy bears, for the children who were being adopted to new families that day.

Today I am a Mom. My kids call me Momala. And I am the Vice President of the United States of America. I am the first woman, the first Indian American, and the first African American to have this important job. I may be the first woman to hold this position, but I won't be the last.

No matter where you come from, no matter what you look like, you can follow your dreams too. We the People are still building a better future, together. We need you, we need all of us, to stand up for what's right.

August 28, 1963: At the historic March on Washington at the Lincoln Memorial in Washington, DC, Dr. Martin Luther King gave a famous speech saying "I Have a Dream" in which children "will not be judged by the color of their skin but by the content of their character."

July 2, 1964: The U.S. Civil Rights Act made it illegal to discriminate on the basis of race, color, religion, sex, or national origin.

October 20, 1964: Kamala Harris was born in Oakland, California.

March 7, 1965: John Lewis led peaceful protestors on a march from Selma to Montgomery, Alabama, protesting for voting rights. Police beat the protestors on "Bloody Sunday." The Constitution gave voting rights for all in 1870, but citizens were still denied their constitutional right to vote in many places. Solidarity marches took place in California throughout the 1960s. Kamala's parents took Kamala, family and friends to the marches and speeches.

August 6, 1965: The Voting Rights Act law made it illegal to create obstacles to keep people from registering and voting.

August 30, 1967: Thurgood Marshall became the first African American to serve as a Supreme Court Justice.

April 4, 1968: Dr. Martin Luther King was murdered. Peaceful protests, and violent riots, took place around the around the world, demanding social justice and an end to war.

1968: Schools around the U.S. make plans to break down racial barriers in schools. Berkeley, California began its own program to integrate elementary schools.

1969: Kamala Harris rode the "Red Rooster" school bus in the second year of the school integration program.

1971: Kamala Harris' parents divorced.

1976: Kamala moved to Montreal, Canada.

1981: Kamala Harris invited a classmate to live with her family, to protect her from abuse at home.

1982: Kamala went to college at Howard University in Washington, D.C., a historically black university where Thurgood Marshall graduated. Kamala joined the debate team, won her first election for student government, and participated in peaceful international protests against Apartheid, the South African policy of racial discrimination.

1986 - 1989: Kamala Harris returned to California to attend and graduate from law school at the University of California Hastings College of the Law.

1988: Kamala grew interested in being a lawyer who works for the public after winning an internship in Oakland, California, at the Alameda County Superior Court.

1990 - 98: Served as Deputy District Attorney for Alameda County, California. She focused on child protection cases.

1994: End of Apartheid and the election of human rights activist Nelson Mandela as President of South Africa.

2000: Harris led the Child and Family Services Unit in San Francisco. She brought teddy bears to her first day of work, for the children being adopted to new families.

2004-2011: Kamala Harris became the first woman elected as the District Attorney of San Francisco, CA.

2008: President Barack Obama was elected President, the first African American President.

2011: Kamala Harris became the first African American and first Indian American woman elected as Attorney General of California. This is the top law job in the most populous U.S. state, with the largest economy in the U.S., and the fifth largest economy in the world.

2014: Married Douglas Emhoff, and became "Momala" to Ella and Cole.

2016: Became the first African American Senator from California and the second African American woman in the U.S. Senate, where she served alongside other members of Congress, including civil rights leader Congressman John Lewis.

January 21, 2019: Entered the 2020 Presidential race on Martin Luther King's birthday.

August 12, 2020: Chosen as Vice Presidential candidate, the first African American woman and South Asian American to run for Vice President on a major party ticket.

November 7, 2020: Was elected Vice President of the United States. Harris tells her 4 year old great niece that she could be President someday.

January 20, 2021: Was inaugurated as the first woman, first African American, and first Asian American Vice President of the United States.

Further Reading

Kamala Harris, *The Truths We Hold: An American Journey* (Young Readers Edition). New York: Philomel Books, 2019.

Kamala Harris, *Super Heroes Are Everywhere*. New York: Philomel Books, 2019.